MW01631230

Genendel Krohn

The Miracles of Chanukah Then & Now

בַּיָּמִים הָהֵם בַּזְּמַן הַזֶּה

illustrated by Tova Katz

FELDHEIM PUBLISHERS
JERUSALEM NEW YORK

ISBN 978-1-59826-645-0

FELDHEIM PUBLISHERS
POB 43163, Jerusalem, Israel
208 Airport Executive Park, Nanuet, NY 10954

www.feldheim.com

10 9 8 7 6 5 4 3 2 1

Printed in Israel

Other titles by Genendel Krohn:

Who is the Builder?
I Wish I Were a King
The Miracle of the Rock and Other Stories
Miracle at Sea and Other Stories
The Miracle of the Golden Dove and Other Stories
The Story of Rabbi Shimon Bar Yochai
The Very Best Gift
When We Left Yerushalayim

Table of Contents

Section 1: BaYamim HaHeim: The Chanukah Story from Our Midrashim and Other Sources

Prologue: The Greeks Come to Eretz Yisrael 6
Chapter 1: Antiochus and His Terrible Decrees 10
Chapter 2: Learning Torah Secretly 12
Chapter 3: Chana and Her Seven Sons 15
Chapter 4: The Jews Fight Back 18
Chapter 5: Yehudis Saves Her People 22
Chapter 6: Beating the Yevanim 25
Chapter 7: The End of Antiochus 28
Chapter 8: The Chanukah Miracle 30

Section 2: BaZman HaZeh: True Chanukah Stories from Recent Times

Chapter 1: Lights on the Train 34
Chapter 2: Saving Lives 36
Chapter 3: Chanukah in Bergen Belsen 39
Chapter 4: A Young Boy's Precious Menorah 42
Chapter 5: Army Secrets 45
Chapter 6: For the Love of a Mitzvah 48

Glossary 52

Dedicated in loving memory
of my grandparents

Rav Avrohom Berger זצ"ל
הרה"ג ר' **אברהם יצחק**
בן הרה"ג ר' **חיים יעקב ישראל** זצ"ל

Mrs. Rochel (Perlstein) Berger ע"ה
הרבנית מרת **רחל** בת ר' **יחיאל מרדכי** ע"ה

ת.נ.צ.ב.ה.

Section One:

BaYamim HaHeim

The Chanukah Story

from Our Midrashim and Other Sources

PROLOGUE

The Greeks Come to Eretz Yisrael

Many years ago, there was a mighty kingdom called Yavan (Greece). Its king was Alexander the Great.

Alexander's greatest wish was to rule over the entire world. His army fought one nation after another and conquered them all. Now he was on his way to Eretz Yisrael.[1]

During that time, the second Beis HaMikdash stood in Yerushalayim. In those days, there was a group of non-Jewish idol worshippers living in Eretz Yisrael. These evil people were known as the Kusim. They were cruel to the Jewish People and often tried to think of ways to hurt them.

When the Kusim heard that Alexander was coming to Eretz Yisrael, they sent a group to meet him. "We have come to warn you about the Jewish People who are planning to start a war against you," lied the Kusim. "We are on your side — let us destroy their Beis HaMikdash!"

When Alexander heard these words, he got so angry at the Jews that he told the Kusim, "I give you permission to do what you want!"

The Kusim were very happy that their evil plan had worked. They marched together with Alexander toward Yerushalayim to help him fight the Jewish People and destroy our precious Beis HaMikdash.

Some Jews found out what the Kusim had done and quickly went to tell the terrible news to Shimon HaTzaddik. Besides being the leader of the Jewish People at that time, Shimon HaTzaddik was also a *kohen gadol*. He put on the eight garments of the *kehunah gedolah*,[2] gathered a large group of leaders among the Bnei Yisrael, and together they set out to meet Alexander. Carrying lit torches in their hands, they walked all night long. Finally, when the sun began to rise, the two groups were able to see each other in the distance.

"Who are those men coming toward us?" asked Alexander.

"Those are the Jews who plan to fight against you," answered the Kusim.

When he got closer, Alexander was able to see the face of Shimon HaTzaddik. The king immediately got out of his carriage and bowed down to him.

Alexander's men were shocked! They said to him, "Why would his royal highness bow down to this Jew?"

"I will tell you the answer," explained Alexander. "Every time I fight and win a war, I see an

[1] תולדות עם עולם, עמ' מ"ז

[2] אברבנאל, מעיני הישועה, מעין ט', תמר ב'

angel that looks exactly like this man." Alexander understood that the *tzaddik* who was standing in front of him somehow helped him to win his wars.

Alexander then turned to the group of Jews and said, "Tell me, why have you come here?"

Shimon HaTzaddik explained, "We have a special house where we pray for you to be successful. Now, some idol-worshippers have convinced you to destroy it!"

Alexander became upset. He wanted to continue winning his wars. "Who would dare to destroy that special house?" he asked.

"It is these Kusim who stand before you," answered Shimon HaTzaddik. "They want to destroy our holy Beis HaMikdash!"

Alexander became furious! He realized that the Kusim had lied to him by saying that the Jews were against him. He said to Shimon, "You have my permission to punish these men!"

Since the Kusim tried to destroy the Beis HaMikdash where we serve Hashem, the place where *they* served idols was destroyed. In addition, the Kusim themselves were also treated harshly.[3]

In the days of Shimon HaTzaddik, the Jewish People served Hashem and were careful to keep the *mitzvos*. Therefore, even though Alexander came to Eretz Yisrael with a mighty army, Hashem did not allow any harm to come to the Jews.

Alexander promised not to destroy the Beis HaMikdash, but he still wanted to see it. Shimon HaTzaddik and the other *Chachamim* led him to Yerushalayim. When Alexander saw the holy palace of Hashem, he said, "Blessed is the G-d of the Jews Who rests in this house! How lucky are the Jews who serve their G-d in this place!"

Alexander then said, "I would like to be remembered here. Please build a golden idol that looks like me, and put it in the Beis HaMikdash. This way, when people see it, they will always think about me."

The *Chachamim* could not believe their ears! What were they going to do? The king would surely kill them if they refused to obey!

Shimon HaTzaddik carefully explained to Alexander that the Torah does not allow idols to be built. "It would be more worthwhile to use your gold to help the *kohanim*," said Shimon HaTzaddik. "But I have another suggestion to make so that your name will be remembered: Any *kohen* who has a baby boy this year will name his son Alexander!"

Alexander liked the idea very much and did not force the Jews to set up an idol. That year, Shimon HaTzaddik's promise was kept, and "Alexander" became a Jewish name.

Alexander was very impressed with the Jewish People and acted kindly toward them.

[3] יומא ס"ט ע"א ומהרש"א שם

Before he left Yerushalayim, he gave a lot of gold and silver to the Jews to fix up the Beis HaMikdash. Then he bowed down to Hashem and left.[4]

Although Alexander the Great did not actually harm the Jewish People with his weapons, he harmed them in a different way. Many of his soldiers remained in Eretz Yisrael. Soon there were Jews who began to copy the Greek way of life, and after a while, they acted more like Greeks than like Jews. This caused Hashem to be unhappy with His people.

[4] יוסיפון, פרק ה'

CHAPTER 1

Antiochus and His Terrible Decrees

King Antiochus was the Greek king who ruled over Eretz Yisrael about 150 years after Alexander the Great. The king wanted everyone to call him Antiochus Epiphanes, which means Antiochus the Great. But he often got drunk and did very strange things. Therefore, many people in his kingdom called him Antiochus Epimanes, which means Antiochus the Crazy. The Jews had a different nickname for him: they called him Antiochus HaRasha because he was very wicked.[1]

Antiochus HaRasha wanted all the people of his land to act like Greeks, without anyone being different. One day, he said to his officers, "I found out that the Jewish People do not bow down to our idols and they follow their own laws. I will send soldiers to Yerushalayim to force them to stop keeping the *mitzvos*!"

Antiochus ordered his general Nikanor to gather a large army, and to go fight against the people of Yerushalayim.

When the Greek soldiers got there, they killed many people. They also went into the Beis HaMikdash and stole all the gold and silver that they could find, including many of the holy *keilim*.[2] When the soldiers discovered the jars of oil that were set aside to be used for the menorah, they broke open the seals, hoping to find gold or pearls inside.[3]

Then the Greek soldiers had the *chutzpah* to build an idol on the holy *mizbe'ach*! On the twenty-fifth day of Kislev, Nikanor and his soldiers brought pigs and other non-kosher animals as *korbanos* in the Beis HaMikdash.

Nikanor announced the new decrees of Antiochus: Anyone caught keeping Shabbos, celebrating Rosh Chodesh, or performing a *bris milah* would be killed! Antiochus also commanded his soldiers to build a *mizbe'ach* for *avodah zarah* in every town and village. He ordered them to bring a pig as a *korban* every single day!

The Jews of Eretz Yisrael learned to keep *mitzvos* in secret. Some Jews escaped from Yerushalayim to other cities in Eretz Yisrael or even to other countries, where there weren't as many Greek officers forcing them to follow the king's decrees.[4]

But there were also many Jews who did listen to Antiochus. Some Jews listened because they wanted to follow the Greek ways. Others listened because they were afraid of getting punished. The people who acted like the Greeks were called by the name *Misyavnim* (Hellenists). When Hashem saw that many Jews were going in the ways of the Greeks, He allowed the Greeks to make even more terrible decrees against His people.

[1] דעת סופרים, עמ' פ"א-פ"ב
[2] תולדות עם עולם, עמ' קנ"א-קנ"ד
[3] שבת כ"א ע"ב וחידושי הר"ן שם
[4] תולדות עם עולם, עמ' קנ"ז-קנ"ט

CHAPTER 2

Learning Torah Secretly

The Greeks knew that what makes us different from all the other nations is our holy Torah. That's why they hated the Torah so much. One day, Antiochus made a terrible decree, forbidding the Jews to gather together to learn Torah.

In those days, the Torah *she-b'al peh* was taught orally by *rebbeim* to their *talmidim*, instead of through *sefarim*. It was only in later years that Torah *she-b'al peh* was written down in the Mishnah and Gemara. Because these *sefarim* were not yet written, the people needed to gather together in order to learn from a *rebbi*. The *rebbi* would read the words of the *Chumash* from little scrolls, and explain the deeper meaning behind the words.

There were many Jews who refused to listen to the Greek orders to stop learning Torah. They would continue learning, no matter what! But how were they to do this without being caught by the Greek officers?

Some Jews decided to live in caves deep inside the mountains, where the Greek soldiers would not easily find them. There they were able to continue to learn Torah, keep Shabbos, and do all the *mitzvos*.[1] Others continued living at home, but they figured out a way to get together and learn without the Greeks catching them.

The following story is an example of what happened many times in Eretz Yisrael during those days.

While a *rebbi* taught Torah in someone's house, one man from the group stood guard by the door. Every day, someone else took a turn doing this very important job. If the guard saw enemy soldiers coming, his job was to run inside and warn everyone about the danger.

One day, as the man was guarding the door, he suddenly heard noises in the distance. Could it be just some leaves rustling in the wind or did he actually hear the stamping of soldiers' feet?

He stood still, waiting for the sounds to come closer. Terrified, he felt his heart beat quickly. Was anyone coming? If there were soldiers, would he be able to warn everyone in time? He knew very well that if the group was caught learning Torah, they'd all be killed.

"Please Hashem," he whispered. "Save us from the terrible *resha'im*!"

A few moments passed. The guard heard voices speaking Greek. They were getting louder. Now he was sure of it — soldiers had come to search for them!

The guard quickly disappeared into the house. "The *Yevanim* are coming!" he cried. "They'll be here any minute!"

[1] יוסיפון, פרק כ'

The men and boys who were learning there quickly hid the Torah scrolls that they had, and took out some spinning tops from their pockets. They had prepared the tops just in case this would happen. They immediately began to spin them.

Moments later, the soldiers entered the house.

"You've gathered here to learn Torah, haven't you?" they yelled. Then the soldiers looked around. They didn't see anyone learning Torah. All they saw was a group of Jews playing with some tops.

"We must have made a mistake," grumbled the soldiers. "We didn't realize you were just playing games in here." As they turned around to leave, they shouted, "Don't even think about learning Torah in here!"

As soon as the soldiers' footsteps could no longer be heard outside, the Jews put their tops back into their pockets, and thanked Hashem for saving their lives. Ignoring the soldiers' words, they continued learning the holy words of the Torah.[2]

Did you know? When we play with a *dreidel* on Chanukah, we remember the great *mesiras nefesh* of the Jews who played with spinning tops and risked their lives in order to learn Torah during this time.

It is the commonly accepted tradition in Eretz Yisrael that the letters on the dreidel are נ (*nun*), ג (*gimmel*), ה (*hei*) , פ (*peh*), which stand for: **נֵס גָּדוֹל הָיָה פֹּה** — *Neis Gadol Hayah Poh*. This means: A great miracle happened here (because these events happened in Eretz Yisrael). Everywhere else in the world, the letters on the dreidel are נ (*nun*), ג (*gimmel*), ה (*hei*), and ש (*shin*), which stand for: **נֵס גָּדוֹל הָיָה שָׁם** — *Neis Gadol Hayah Sham*. This means: A great miracle happened there.

Since the *Yevanim* tried to stop us from learning Torah and keeping *mitzvos*, it is proper to learn a lot of Torah on Chanukah.[3] Parents give Chanukah *gelt* (money) to their children to reward them for having learned well in the past, and to encourage them to learn well in the future.[4]

[2] אוצר כל מנהגי ישורון, סי׳ י״ט, אות ד׳ (עמ׳ 57)

[3] של״ה, מסכת תמיד, פרק דרך חיים תוכחת מוסר א׳

[4] שפתי חיים, מועדים ב׳, עמ׳ קל״ד, בשם הרב מפונוביז׳

CHAPTER 3

Chana and Her Seven Sons

There was a woman named Chana who had seven sons. They feared only Hashem, and followed the *mitzvos* even when it was dangerous to do so. One day, the Greek soldiers arrested Chana and her sons and brought them to the king's palace.

First, the oldest son was brought to Antiochus. Near the king stood a large idol. "Bow down to my idol or you will die!" ordered the king.

"I cannot do that," declared the oldest son. "The Torah says: 'אָנֹכִי ה' אֱלֹקֶיךָ — I am Hashem your G-d,' and so I cannot serve anyone besides Him." The soldiers took the boy away and killed him.

Then they brought Chana's second son before the king. "Bow down to my idol!" commanded the king.

The young man answered proudly, "I will not bow down to your idol because the Torah says: 'לֹא יִהְיֶה לְךָ... — You shall not serve idols.'" The soldiers took the boy away and killed him.

The third son was brought next. "Bow down to my idol!" said the king. "No, I will not!" announced the child. The soldiers took this boy, too, and killed him.

The same thing happened when they brought the next three sons. They all refused to bow down, and willingly gave up their lives *al kiddush Hashem.*

Finally, the youngest son, who was still a small child, was brought into the room. Antiochus said to him, "Little boy, bow down to my idol!" The young child did not become afraid. He looked at the king and said, "Hashem promised that He won't trade *us* for any other nation. We promised that we won't trade *Him* for any other G-d. I cannot bow down to your idol."

By now, the king was very embarrassed. All those children had dared to disobey him! Why weren't they afraid of him?

Suddenly, the king thought of an idea. "Come here, little boy," he said softly. "Let's make a deal. I will throw my ring next to the idol and you will bend down to pick it up. That way, it will look like you are bowing down to the idol, even though you are really not."

"Absolutely not!" announced the little boy. "Even pretending to bow down to an idol would be disrespectful to Hashem!"

The king got angry and told his soldiers to kill the child.

As the soldiers led the little boy away, Chana begged them, "Please let me give my son one last kiss before he dies!"

When the soldiers agreed, Chana went to her youngest son, and hugged and kissed him. Then she said, "My dear child, when you get to *Shamayim*, I want you to go to Avraham Avinu and tell him that I said, '*You* were willing to give up one son for Hashem, but *I* gave up seven!'"

After this last son was taken away, Chana also died. When her *neshamah* went to *Shamayim*, a *bas kol* called out, "אֵם הַבָּנִים שְׂמֵחָה — This mother is happy and proud!" The voice from *Shamayim* was announcing to all that Chana was happy when she saw the great reward that her children received because of what they had done. She was proud that her children had not been afraid to give up their lives *al kiddush Hashem.*[1]

[1] גיטין נ"ז ע"ב; איכה רבה, פרשה א', פיסקה נ'; מדרש ר' דוד הנגיד, וישב, עמ' קע"ה-קע"ז

CHAPTER 4

The Jews Fight Back

Greek soldiers walked up and down the streets of Yerushalayim, making sure the people obeyed the commands of King Antiochus. Each day, it became more and more difficult for the Jews to follow the Torah.

There was a family of *kohanim* known as the Chashmona'im. The father of the family was Mattisyahu, the son of Yochanan the *kohen gadol*. Mattisyahu had five sons: Yehuda, Shimon, Yochanan, Yonasan, and Elazar. All of them were very big *tzaddikim*.

When the Chashmona'im saw how difficult it was to keep the *mitzvos* in Yerushalayim, they moved to a nearby town called Modi'in, where there were fewer soldiers around. But before long, the Greek soldiers followed them there.[1]

One day, the Jews of Modi'in were ordered to gather in the center of the town. Among the people who gathered there were the five sons of the Chashmona'im family and their elderly father, Mattisyahu.[2]

The soldiers called out, "Mattisyahu! You are an important man! We command you to bring a *korban* to our idol so that everyone will see! If you do not do so, you will be killed!"

Mattisyahu was not afraid of the wicked men. He feared only Hashem. "I will not serve an idol," he announced to everyone, "even if I must die!"

The soldiers became angry. They were about to punish him when all of a sudden, a *Misyaven* (a Jew who acted like the Greeks) walked over to the *mizbe'ach* and began to bring a *korban* to the idol.

Mattisyahu knew that this Jew deserved to die for doing such a terrible *aveirah*, so he took out a sword and killed him. Afterwards, Mattisyahu's sons helped him kill the Greek soldiers who were there, and together, they broke the *mizbe'ach* that had been built for the idol.

Then Mattisyahu called out, "מִי לַה' אֵלָי! — *Mi laHashem eilai!* Whoever is on Hashem's side, come to me!"[3] Those were the same words that Moshe Rabbeinu used when he wanted to punish the people who had sinned with the *eigel ha-zahav*, the golden calf.

Many Jews gathered around Mattisyahu. They knew that the time had come to fight back against the *Yevanim*. They left their homes and went to live in caves in the desert where they were free to learn Torah and do *mitzvos*. At night, they left their caves to go and destroy any *mizbe'ach* they found that had been set up for idols.

Mattisyahu and his men traveled from town to town, fighting against the soldiers in each place and performing *bris milahs* on baby boys whose parents had been too afraid to give their children

1 תולדות עם עולם, עמ' קס"ז
2 יוסיפון, פרק כ'
3 דעת סופרים, עמ' ק"ג

a *bris*. This group gave people the courage to keep the *mitzvos* of Hashem. It also gave them the courage to fight back against their enemies.

Wherever Mattisyahu went, more people joined his small army. The war against Yavan had begun.

One day, Yochanan, the son of Mattisyahu, traveled to Yerushalayim. He took a small sword and hid it under his clothing so that no one would see it. With the sword tucked away, he went to the Greek army camp and said to the guards, "My name is Yochanan. I have come to speak with your master."

The guards went to the general Nikanor and told him, "Yochanan, the son of Mattisyahu, is here to speak with you."

"Send him in to me at once!" commanded Nikanor.

When Yochanan entered Nikanor's tent, the general said, "I know that you are among the group that has rebelled against the king. Why have you come here today?"

"I have decided to switch sides and join the Greek army," answered Yochanan slyly.

"It's hard for me to know if you are telling the truth," said Nikanor. "But I have a way to test you. If you will bring a pig as a *korban* inside the Beis HaMikdash, then I will know for sure that you are on my side. Are you willing to do that?"

"Sure," answered Yochanan. "But there's one problem. There are many soldiers all around. I am worried that if they see me do that, they will tell the Jews what I have done, and then the Jews will kill me.

"Therefore," continued Yochanan, "I can bring up the pig on one condition. You must first send everyone away from the Beis HaMikdash so that no one will see me."

"That sounds like a good idea," agreed the general. "I will do as you ask." He was very excited for a member of the Chashmona'im family to join his army.

When the two men entered the Beis HaMikdash, Nikanor ordered all his soldiers to leave the area. Now Nikanor was left without anyone to protect him.

Yochanan whispered a *tefillah* asking Hashem to help him. Then he drew his sword and killed the mighty general. Yochanan looked up to *Shamayim* and said, "Please Hashem, don't consider it an *aveirah* that I killed this *rasha* inside the holy Beis HaMikdash. I beg of You, please help us win against the rest of his men."

Yochanan ran outside and blew a *shofar* to gather the Jews together to fight.

When the soldiers realized that the Jews were ready to attack, they ran to get Nikanor so he could lead them in battle. But when they went into the Beis HaMikdash, they saw that he was dead! Now the *Yevanim* were left without a general to lead them! The Greek soldiers

became so confused that they started to kill one another. The Jews killed many Greek soldiers as well. Hashem caused the few to win against the many![4]

Even though this battle against the Greeks had been won, Antiochus did not remove his terrible decrees. It was still dangerous to keep the *mitzvos*, and it was still impossible for the Jews to go to the Beis HaMikdash. More battles needed to be fought before the Jews would be free to serve Hashem once again in the Beis HaMikdash.

Did you know? The first three letters of the Hebrew name "חַשְׁמוֹנָאִים — Chashmona'im" remind us of the three main *mitzvos* that the *Yevanim* forbade the Jews to keep. The letters ח (*ches*), ש (*shin*), and מ (*mem*) stand for חֹדֶשׁ — (*Rosh*) *Chodesh*, שַׁבָּת — *Shabbos*, and מִילָה — (*Bris*) *Milah*. The Chashmona'im fought against the *Yevanim* in order to make sure that these *mitzvos* would continue to be kept by the Jewish People.[5]

4 מגילת אנטיוכוס, פס' ט"ו-כ"ה; ילקוט מעם לועז, בהעלותך ח', א'-ב' (עמ' צ"ב)
5 פרי צדיק בשם האריז"ל, מקץ, אות י"ד

CHAPTER 5

Yehudis Saves Her People

There was a powerful Greek general at that time named Elipornee. He was very evil and thought of a cruel plan to destroy the Jewish People.

Elipornee and his soldiers surrounded the city of Yerushalayim. Around Yeurshalayim there were pipes, or aqueducts, that brought water from the mountains into the city. Elipornee and his men broke these water pipes!

"In a few weeks," said Elipornee, "the Jews will run out of water and will die of thirst. Then we'll be able to get into the city without a fight. Soldiers, you must guard the streams in the mountains and kill anyone who comes out of the city to get water!"

Slowly, the water in Yerushalayim ran out. After twenty days, there was barely anything left to drink. The people said, "Let's give up!"

They went into the Beis HaMikdash and began to cry. "We know that we have sinned to You, Hashem," they said. "But please save us from our enemies!"

With tears in his eyes, the general Uziyahu announced, "Let's wait five more days to see if Hashem will save us. If He doesn't save us by then, we'll give ourselves over to the enemy."

There was a widow named Yehudis who lived in Yerushalayim at that time. Yehudis was a big *tzadekes*. When she heard Uziyahu's words, she became upset. "You must continue to trust in Hashem," she told him. "Do not give up!"

Yehudis then said to the Jewish generals, "I have a plan which could save us from Elipornee. But I need you to *daven* that the plan should work." The generals listened to her plan and promised to *daven* for her.

That evening, Yehudis got dressed in her fanciest clothing and wore her most expensive jewelry. She put some food into a bag and handed it to her lady servant. The two women walked together through the gates of the city, toward the enemy camp. They continued walking all night long. In the morning, the enemy soldiers noticed them.

"Who goes there?" called the soldiers.

"My name is Yehudis," the *tzadekes* answered calmly. "I am a Jew who has escaped from Yerushalayim because I know that you're going to win this war. I decided to join your side so that I can help you." This was part of her plan.

The soldiers believed Yehudis and brought her to their general. Yehudis said to Elipornee, "Hashem sent me to tell you that you are going to win this war. The Jews have sinned and deserve to be punished. I ran away from Yerushalayim to give you this message." Even though this was not true, Yehudis was allowed to say this in order to save the Jewish People.

Elipornee was very happy when he heard these words. "You may stay here with us," he told Yehudis.

"Thank you!" she said. "I have just one request. Please allow me to go outside the camp three times a day in order to pray to my G-d. That way, He will continue to speak to me, and He will tell me the best time for you to attack."

"That is not a problem," said the general. "My guards will allow you to go in and out of the camp as often as you'd like."

Yehudis was given a place to stay inside the enemy camp. Three times a day, she left the camp and begged Hashem to help her with her plan.

On the third day, Elipornee invited Yehudis to a private party. Now was her chance! She reached into her bag and took out some food made from salty cheese. Then she served it to the general. The cheese made him very thirsty. When he asked for a drink, she poured him one cup of wine after another. The general drank more and more wine until he became so tired that he fell into a very deep sleep. While her lady servant guarded the door, Yehudis grabbed Elipornee's sword which was hanging on a pole nearby. With a *tefillah* on her lips, she killed the mighty general.[1]

Yehudis quickly left the room and closed the door behind her. She and her servant left the Greek camp and nobody stopped them because they had special permission to do so.

The two women walked as fast as they could until they finally reached the gates of Yerushalayim. When they arrived, Yehudis told the Jewish soldiers how Hashem had helped her to kill Elipornee. The people were filled with happiness and thanked Hashem for this great miracle.

Early the next morning, Uziyahu led his men toward the enemy camp, and made a surprise attack. The Greek soldiers quickly ran to wake up Elipornee so he could lead them in battle! They knocked on Elipornee's door, but no one answered. When they finally opened the door, they were shocked to find him lying there dead!

The soldiers suddenly became afraid. Without Elipornee to lead them, they no longer had the courage to fight! They ran away as fast as they could while the Jewish army chased after them. The Jews were able to kill thousands of Greek soldiers and they won the battle! Once again, Hashem caused the weak to win against the strong![2]

Did you know? Since the miracle of winning the war happened through a woman, and since some of the terrible decrees of Antiochus were against women, the custom is for women to celebrate Chanukah in an extra way. They do not do certain types of work during the first half hour after the menorah is lit. This includes sewing and doing laundry.[3]

Some people eat dairy food on Chanukah to remember the miracle that Hashem made for Yehudis after she served Elipornee cheese.[4]

1 כל בו, סי' מ"ד
2 ילקוט מעם לועז, בהעלותך ח', א'-ב' (עמ' צ"ה-ק"א)
3 שו"ע, או"ח, סי' תר"ע, סעי' א'
4 רמ"א שם, סעי' ב'

CHAPTER 6

Beating the Yevanim

One day, Antiochus decided to get rid of the Jewish army, once and for all! He called Bagris, his top general, and ordered him to go and fight against the Jews.

Bagris had already been to Eretz Yisrael once before to fight against the Chashmona'im. But he had become so frightened in battle that he quickly got on a ship and returned to Yavan. Now Antiochus wanted to send him again.

Bagris was very afraid. He said, "Your Majesty, we will not be able to fight against the five sons of Mattisyahu. They are too strong for us. The only way we can hope to win is if you order many more thousands of soldiers to join our army. Then, with an army that size, there's a chance that we will win."

Antiochus followed the advice of his general and ordered a huge army to go to war. When Bagris saw how many people had come to help him fight, he was no longer afraid to attack the Jews. He took the soldiers as well as many war elephants, and set out to fight against the Chashmona'im.[1]

In those days, elephants were used to help armies fight their wars. Soldiers sat inside of a tower that stood on top of the elephant's back. The soldiers shot arrows at the people below, while they themselves were protected inside the tower.

[1] מגילת אנטיוכוס, פס' מ"ג-מ"ח

Bagris arrived in Eretz Yisrael and tried to ruin the Beis HaMikdash by making thirteen holes in its walls. When he saw the small Jewish army, he called out, "You fools! How do you dare to fight against our huge and mighty army?"

The Jews began to get scared. They looked to see if perhaps a strong army would come from another country to save them. When their leaders saw this, they said, "Do not put your trust in people to save you! Put your trust in Hashem!"

"You are right," exclaimed the people. "We will rely only on Hashem!" They fasted and *davened* to Hashem to save them from their enemies.

When a non-Jewish army fights a war, the soldiers make sure to eat big meals that day in order to be strong. But in those days, our soldiers did just the opposite. They fasted and *davened* for help from Hashem.[2]

Elazar, the youngest son of Mattisyahu, noticed that one of the enemy's elephants was decorated with the king's royal sign. Elazar was sure that the king was inside the tower on its back. Elazar knew that if the king died, this would help the Jews win the war.

Elazar bravely ran toward the elephant, went underneath it, and stuck a spear into its belly. The elephant died and fell on top of Elazar, killing him. The people riding on top of the elephant also fell down and died. But unfortunately, Elazar had made a mistake; the king was not among them.

At this point, Hashem gathered the seventy *malachim* in *Shamayim* who are in charge of the seventy nations of the world. He ordered the *malachim* to help the Jewish People win the war. "Kill the Greek army!" Hashem commanded them.

When the Greeks shot their arrows, the *malachim* turned the arrows around, and they bounced right back at the soldiers who shot them. At the same time, Hashem caused loud and scary noises to come from *Shamayim* and frighten the Greeks. He also sent down fiery hail and lightning which hit the soldiers and burnt them up.[3] One by one, the soldiers were killed until almost the entire army was gone. The mighty Bagris was also killed in the war. Hashem caused the *tzaddikim* to win against the *resha'im.*[4]

2 משנה ברורה, סי' תרפ"ו, ס"ק ב'

3 מדרש ר' דוד הנגיד, וישב, עמ' קפ"א

4 ילקוט מעם לועז, בהעלותך ח', א'-ב' (עמ' צ"ג-צ"ד)

CHAPTER 7

The End of Antiochus

While Bagris was fighting the war in Eretz Yisrael, Antiochus heard about a very rich city in Persia where Alexander the Great had hidden many of his treasures. He led a small group of soldiers there and surrounded the city, hoping to conquer it and steal all the riches. The people of that city were very strong. They fought against him and chased him all the way to the land of Bavel.[1]

[1] תולדות עם עולם ח"ב, עמ' קע"ג-קע"ד

Soon after Antiochus lost the battle in Persia, messengers came and told him that his great army had lost the war in Eretz Yisrael. When Antiochus heard this, he became sick from sorrow. Hashem punished him further by sending him a terrible sickness that caused him a lot of pain. This sickness also caused his body to give off a horrible smell.

One day, as Antiochus was riding his royal carriage, the horses suddenly became afraid. They started pulling the carriage in different directions until the carriage turned over and the king fell out. Many of the bones in his body broke, and he screamed for help. Since he had such a terrible smell, no one wanted to come close to him! His soldiers ran away and left him to die alone.

As Antiochus HaRasha lay there dying, he said, "I know that Hashem is punishing me for fighting against the Jews and making their Beis HaMikdash *tamei*. That's why He made me suffer so much and die in this faraway land." [2]

Did you know? Yehuda became the leader of the Jewish army after his father Mattisyahu died. People called him Yehuda HaMaccabee. The word "*Maccabee*" means strong.[3] It also stands for the words "**מִי כָמֹכָה בָּאֵלִם י-י** — *Mi Chamocha Ba'eilim Hashem* — Who is like You among the strong ones, Hashem." Yehuda put those words onto his flag for all to see, so that everyone would realize that it was not his own strength but rather Hashem's strength which caused him to win the wars.

Even though Yehuda was the first to be called by the name Maccabee, people soon began to use the name Maccabim when they spoke about the Chashmona'im. The Maccabim never forgot that Hashem was the One Who was fighting their battles.

Some say that the word Maccabee also stands for Mattisyahu Kohen Ben Yochanan.[4]

[2] מדרש ר' דוד הנגיד, מקץ, עמ' קצ"ז
[3] יוסיפון, פרק כ'
[4] תולדות עם עולם, עמ' ק"ע

CHAPTER 8

The Chanukah Miracle

After winning the war against the Greek armies, Yehuda led his men straight to Yerushalayim and chased away the Greek soldiers who were still there. It was the twenty-fifth day of Kislev, exactly three years after Antiochus' soldiers had gone into the Beis HaMikdash and made it *tamei.*

As the small Jewish army climbed up to Har HaBayis, they were so happy — they would finally be able to serve Hashem once again in the Beis HaMikdash!

But when they looked around and saw what the enemy had done to the holy palace of Hashem, they became sad and tore their clothes in mourning. They immediately got to work cleaning the Beis HaMikdash and getting rid of anything that was *tamei.* They wanted to begin doing the *avodah* again as soon as possible.

Yehuda chose *kohanim* to purify the Beis HaMikdash. They replaced the *shulchan*, as well as other *keilim* that the *Yevanim* had stolen. They fixed the walls and tiles that had been broken, and hung up the *paroches*, the curtain that separates the *Heichal* from the *Kodesh HaKodashim.*[1] When they saw that the holy *mizbe'ach* had been used for idols, they understood that it had become *tamei* and could no longer be used. They broke it apart, storing the pieces in a room of the Beis HaMikdash, and built a new one in its place.[2]

The Jewish People made a *chanukas ha-mizbe'ach*, a celebration in honor of the new *mizbe'ach.* They brought many *korbanos* on the new *mizbe'ach* to thank Hashem for helping them win the wars. They celebrated their happiness with music and singing.

When Yehuda and his men looked for the gold menorah in order to light it, it was nowhere to be found. Realizing that it had been stolen by the Greeks, they quickly began to build a new menorah with seven branches. Since Antiochus had stolen all the gold from the Beis HaMikdash, they could not make the new menorah out of gold. Instead, they made it out of iron and covered it with tin. (Years later, when the Jewish People had more money, they made a new menorah out of silver. When the Jews had even more money, they made a new one out of gold.)[3]

The next problem was that they could not find any *tahor* oil with which to light the menorah. They searched one room after another, but they soon realized that all the oil had been made *tamei* by the *Yevanim.* The Chashmona'im were very sad. There is a mitzvah to light the menorah in the Beis HaMikdash every evening, and they wanted to light in the best way possible — with *tahor* oil.

1 תולדות עם עולם, עמ' קע"ה-קע"ו
2 עבודה זרה נ"ב ע"ב
3 עבודה זרה מ"ג ע"א

Suddenly, someone cried out, "Look! I found a *pach shemen*! I found a jar of oil with the seal of the *kohen gadol* still on it!"

"We have *tahor* oil after all!" everyone called excitedly. "Now we will be able to light the menorah!"

Although the Chashmona'im were very happy to find the jar of oil, they were disappointed when they saw that the jar had enough oil to last for only one night. They knew it would take seven days to get new *tahor* oil! What would they use in the menorah until then?

Hashem saw their disappointment. He knew that the Chashmona'im had fought against the *Yevanim* in order to be able to serve Him properly once again. If not for them, the Torah and *mitzvos* would have been forgotten from the Jewish People because of Antiochus' terrible decrees![4] Hashem wanted to show His special love for them so He made one more miracle: the small amount of oil lasted for eight nights, until the new oil was ready to be used! When the *Chachamim* of that time saw that Hashem made this great *neis* for them, they decided to make those eight days into a *Yom Tov*. That *Yom Tov* is called Chanukah.

For eight days beginning with the twenty-fifth day of Kislev, Jews all over the world light the menorah with happiness and joy, and thank Hashem for the great miracles that He made for us![5]

Did you know? The name Chanukah comes from the words "חָנוּ כ"ה — *Chanu chof hey*," which means, "They rested on the twenty-fifth day." On the twenty-fifth day of Kislev, the Jews rested from their wars against the *Yevanim*.[6]

The name Chanukah also comes from the words *chanukas ha-mizbe'ach*. During the days of Chanukah, they were finally able to fix up the Beis HaMikdash and bring *korbanos* once again on their new *mizbe'ach*.[7] That was the exact same date that Moshe Rabbeinu finished building the Mishkan many years earlier.[8]

Even though the menorah in the Beis HaMikdash had seven lights, the Chanukah menorahs in our homes have eight lights in order to remember the miracle that the oil burned for eight nights. It's best to light the menorah with olive oil because the *neis* happened with olive oil.[9]

On Chanukah, we eat oily foods such as *latkes* and donuts in order to remember the miracle that Hashem made with the jar of oil.

4 רמב"ן, ויחי, פ' מ"ט, פס' י'
5 שבת כ"א ע"ב
6 ספר אבודרהם, חנוכה
7 אור זרוע, ח"ב, הל' חנוכה, סי' שכ"א
8 במדבר רבה, נשא, פרשה י"ג, פיסקה ב'
9 רמ"א, או"ח, סי' תרע"ג, סעי' א'

Section Two:

BaZman HaZeh

True Chanukah Stories from Recent Times

CHAPTER 1

Lights on the Train

It was the end of Chanukah in 1938 when the Geier family got on a train to leave their home forever. Jews were no longer wanted in Germany, and so the Geiers decided to move to another country.

Carrying their suitcases and passports, Mr. and Mrs. Geier boarded the train in Berlin, Germany, together with their son and daughter. They *davened* to Hashem to help them get to Holland safely, so that they would be able to live a life of Torah and *mitzvos* in freedom.

While the train traveled past cities and fields, Mr. Geier watched as the sun went down and the sky turned black. It was the eighth night of Chanukah and he wanted so badly to light the menorah. But since there were many Germans on the train, Mr. Geier was afraid that if he lit the menorah, they would realize he was a Jew and he would be punished.

The lights in the train turned on as the world around them grew dark. Mrs. Geier was able to see the sadness on her husband's face. "I know you feel bad that you can't light the menorah tonight," she whispered. "Hashem will surely forgive you." But Mr. Geier was still sad. He did not want to miss the chance to do this special mitzvah.

As the train got to the border between Germany and Holland, it began to slow down until it came to a full stop. At the station, the German officers would need to check all the people's passports to make sure that they were allowed to cross the border. As the officers went from person to person, there suddenly was a blackout and all the lights in the train went off. It was pitch black in there! Babies began to cry. People became afraid. No one knew what to do.

A few people lit matches which gave a tiny bit of light for just a couple of seconds. This was Mr. Geier's chance. He quickly stood up and felt around until he found his coat. He reached inside the pocket and pulled out nine candles. Carefully, he set up eight candles and a *shamash* near the windowsill next to him. He quietly said the *berachos* and lit the candles. When he finished, he sat down, a big smile on his face.

All of a sudden, someone called out excitedly, "Look! There's light over there!" The German officers came closer to Mr. Geier's candles. "What a great idea to bring along travel candles!" they said to him.

The officers used the light of the candles to check the people's passports in that part of the train. When the Chanukah candles had burned for half an hour — the exact amount of time needed to fulfill the mitzvah — the lights in the train suddenly went back on. The officers left to finish their work in other parts of the train.

When all the passports had been checked, the train was finally allowed to cross the border to safety. Mr. Geier thanked Hashem for bringing his family to freedom and also for making a special Chanukah miracle just for him.

CHAPTER 2
Saving Lives

Solly Ganor was an eleven-year-old-boy living in Kovno, Lithuania in 1939. Solly loved Chanukah. He loved lighting the menorah and singing Chanukah songs. He loved playing *dreidel* and eating *latkes*. He loved getting together with all his relatives at the family Chanukah party. And he loved getting Chanukah *gelt* from his parents and sometimes even from his aunts and uncles.

On the first night of Chanukah after the candles had been lit, Solly decided to visit his Aunt Anushka in the fancy store that she owned. Many rich people shopped in her store because she sold expensive foods from all over the world, which couldn't be found anywhere else in Lithuania.

When Solly walked into the store, Aunt Anushka was helping a non-Jewish man with slanted eyes. As soon as she noticed her nephew, she called out, "Solly, come and meet Mr. Sugihara." Then she explained, "This important man is from Japan and he is in charge of the Japanese government office here in Lithuania."

Solly walked over to the man and shook his hand. Mr. Sugihara smiled kindly.

"Let me give you some Chanukah *gelt*," said Aunt Anushka. When Mr. Sugihara saw the woman give a coin to her nephew, he too held out a coin. "Since tonight is Chanukah," he said, "I will act like an uncle and give you some money too." He handed the coin to Solly.

Solly thanked the man and took the coin. Then he said something that surprised even himself. "If you are my uncle," said Solly, "then you must come to our family Chanukah party!"

Aunt Anushka gave Solly a look. He knew what she was thinking: *How could you invite this non-Jewish man to your Chanukah party?* Solly himself didn't know why he did it. But now it was too late.

"Thank you very much for inviting me!" said Mr. Sugihara. "I've never been to a Chanukah party before! I'd love to come!" Solly told him when and where it would be, and the important Japanese man promised to come to the party which would take place a few days later.

When Solly got back home that night, he found out that guests had moved into his house. A Jewish man named Mr. Rosenblatt had escaped with his daughter from Poland, where World War II was being fought. Since Mr. Rosenblatt and his daughter were left with no place to live, Solly's parents invited them to stay in their house.

A few days later, Solly's aunts, uncles, and cousins came to his house for the family Chanukah party. Of course, Mr. Rosenblatt and his daughter were there too. In the middle of the party, Mr. and Mrs. Sugihara arrived.

The Sugiharas watched carefully as Mr. Ganor and Solly lit their menorahs and sang Chanukah songs. Mr. Sugihara asked a lot of questions. He learned about the Maccabim and about the miracle Hashem made when the flames of the menorah burned for eight nights.

In the middle of the party, Mr. Rosenblatt decided to speak to Mr. Sugihara. He told the important Japanese officer how terribly the Jews were suffering in Poland. The room became quiet because everyone wanted to hear what he was saying. In the middle of talking, Mr. Rosenblatt started to cry. Everyone felt sorry for him.

Mr. Rosenblatt begged the Japanese officer to get him a visa. A visa is a very important official paper which is needed in order to travel from one country to another. Mr. Rosenblatt wanted a visa so he could move to another country, far away from where the war was being fought. Mr. Sugihara told him to come to his office the next morning, and promised he would try to help.

The Sugiharas enjoyed the Chanukah party very much. Before leaving, Mr. Sugihara said, "It was very special meeting all of you. I would love to meet more people from the Jewish community."

Six months later, the German army came to Lithuania. A lot of people in Lithuania tried to leave the country which was now in the middle of a war. But no one would give them visas, and so they could not leave. Many Jews went to Mr. Sugihara and asked him for visas. Mr. Sugihara worked very hard to help them. He saved the entire Mir Yeshiva and thousands of other Jews by giving them visas to Japan. Today, there are over 40,000 Jews who are children and grandchildren of the people who got visas to Japan. They are all alive today because of Mr. Sugihara's efforts.

A few years ago, Mrs. Sugihara wrote a book about her husband. In her book, she wrote that one of the reasons her husband liked the Jews and tried to save them was because of a young boy named Solly Ganor. A beautiful family Chanukah party caused an important Japanese officer to care about the Jewish People and to save thousands of Jewish lives.

CHAPTER 3

Chanukah in Bergen Belsen

"Did you hear the news?" one Jewish prisoner asked his friend in a whisper. "The Rebbe will be lighting the menorah tonight — in his room! Everyone is invited to come and join him!"

It was going to be the first night of Chanukah in the Bergen Belsen concentration camp during World War II. For weeks, the Jewish prisoners had been waiting and planning for this big night.

The Nazis treated the Jews in the camps like slaves. There was never enough food to eat, surely not to put away and save. How, then, would the Jews get oil for the menorah? And where would they find wicks to light?

When a wooden shoe was found, the Bluzhever Rebbe, Rav Yisrael Spira, decided to use it as a menorah. The Jewish prisoners pulled threads out of their uniforms. Twisting them together, they made the threads into wicks. But where would they find oil? A small amount

3015

of black shoe polish was snuck out of the shoe factory where one of the Jewish prisoners worked. The shoe polish would be used instead of oil.

When it was time to light the Chanukah candles, the Jewish prisoners secretly entered the Rebbe's room one by one, making sure not to be seen by the Nazi soldiers.

With a room packed with people, the Bluzhever Rebbe began to sing the *berachos* of "לְהַדְלִיק נֵר שֶׁל חֲנֻכָּה — *L'hadlik neir shel Chanukah*" and "שֶׁעָשָׂה נִסִּים — *She'asah nisim.*"

He was about to say the third *berachah* of *She'hecheyanu* when he stopped. He turned to look at the large crowd that had gathered, and smiled. Then, in a strong voice, he sang the *berachah.*

The Jewish prisoners were filled with joy at having the opportunity to join in this great mitzvah of lighting the menorah. They thanked the Rebbe for making it happen.

As the people were leaving, one Jew went over to the Rebbe. "I have a question to ask," said the man. "How were you able to say the *berachah* of *She'hecheyanu?* This *berachah* thanks Hashem for keeping us alive. But it's hard to feel happy to be alive when we're suffering so much in this camp."

"That's a very good question," answered the Rebbe. "In fact, I myself had that very same question and that's why I stopped before saying the *berachah.*

"And then I looked around. I saw Jews of all types — some who keep the *mitzvos* and some who don't. Yet they all gathered here to be part of the mitzvah of lighting the Chanukah menorah, even though they knew that if they were caught, they would be punished. When I saw everyone here, I felt so proud to be part of such a holy nation! I thought to myself that it's worth being alive just to see such a group!"

Slowly, the Jewish prisoners snuck back to their own rooms, filled with happiness and hope. They thought about how Hashem had saved the Jewish People from their enemies in the times of Chanukah, and they *davened* that Hashem would save them too from their enemies. They looked forward to the time when they'd be able to light the menorah again without any fear.

CHAPTER 4

A Young Boy's Precious Menorah

Mr. Winneger was a Jewish soldier who fought in the American army during World War II. After the war was over, many American soldiers stayed in Europe for a few more months to make sure everything was in order.

One night, as Mr. Winneger was walking outside a small village, he noticed a boy running. The boy was holding something large in his hands, and the soldier was afraid it might be dangerous. When the boy saw the soldier, he tried to hide what he was holding inside of his coat.

Mr. Winneger began to run after the boy. The boy ran quickly, and as he ran, the object he was carrying fell to the ground. The boy stopped and turned back to get it, but the Jewish soldier had already picked it up. It was a beautiful silver menorah! The boy tried to grab it away, saying, "Give it to me! It's mine!"

Mr. Winneger immediately returned the menorah to the boy. "You do not need to be afraid of me," said the soldier. "I'm a Jew just like you."

Mr. Winneger spoke to him for a long time, and soon the boy realized that he could trust the kind Jewish soldier. The boy told the soldier that his name was Dovid. His father had been killed at the beginning of the war, and his mother had probably been killed too.

"Where did you get this special menorah?" asked Mr. Winneger.

"It was my father's menorah," answered the boy. "When the war was over, I went back to my house. Non-Jews were living there and they told me to go away. I begged them to give me my father's menorah, and they agreed."

"Why did you want the menorah more than anything else?" asked Mr. Winneger.

"You see," said Dovid, "this menorah has been in my family for over two hundred years. I remember when my grandfather would light it, and then after he died, my father lit it. The menorah was very special to our family, and we were always very proud of it. That's why I wanted to keep it."

The more time Mr. Winneger spent with Dovid, the more he grew to like him. He took care of the young boy, giving him clothing to wear and food to eat. When the army finally told the soldiers that they could return to America, Mr. Winneger decided to take Dovid with him.

Dovid happily agreed and went to live in New York together with his new friend who had become like a father to him. Of course, Dovid brought his precious menorah along with him.

Whenever Mr. Winneger's friends would come to visit, he proudly showed them Dovid's beautiful menorah. One friend offered to pay thousands of dollars for the special menorah, but Dovid wouldn't sell it for any amount of money. This was the only thing that he had left

from his family and he wanted to keep it forever.

When Chanukah came, Dovid polished his precious menorah. He said the *berachos* and proudly lit the very same menorah that his father and grandfather had lit.

One night of Chanukah, a little while after the candles had been lit, there was a knock at the door. Dovid was upstairs learning at the time.

When Mr. Winneger opened the door, he found a woman standing there. "I was walking outside," she explained, "when I saw your menorah in the window. The menorah looks exactly like the one that my husband lit before the war. I have never seen any other menorah similar to it.

"The menorah we owned had been in our family for over two hundred years," she continued. "But now it's gone. Would you mind if I come inside to look at your special menorah?"

Mr. Winneger invited the woman into his house, and as she stared at the silver menorah, he quickly ran upstairs and asked Dovid to come down.

When Dovid entered the room, he saw a woman gently touching his precious menorah. "May I help you?" he asked.

The woman turned around. Dovid looked at her face. "Mama!" he cried. "I can't believe it's you! I didn't know you were still alive!"

Too shocked to speak, the woman hugged her son tightly as tears rolled down both of their cheeks. In the most unexpected way, the mitzvah of lighting the menorah helped bring a mother and her son back together.

CHAPTER 5

Army Secrets

For many years, Jews were not able to *daven* at the Kosel HaMa'aravi because the Arabs did not allow them to go there. Then, in 1967, the Six Day War broke out. For six days, Hashem made amazing miracles and the Israeli army won against their Arab enemies. We got back many parts of Eretz Yisrael, including the Kosel. Jews were once again free to *daven* at the holiest place in the world.

During the war, the Israeli army captured a group of important Arab officers from Egypt. Even after the war was over, these enemy officers were kept in prison. The Israeli soldiers asked them a lot of questions in order to learn secrets about the Egyptian army. Some officers gave away the secrets immediately. Others were tougher, and it took a lot of time before they began to give information. But there was one Egyptian officer who would not give away any secrets at all. His name was Gamal Kareem. Gamal remained loyal to his Arab leaders and refused to say anything that might harm them. When the Israeli officers asked him questions, he sat quietly without saying a word. He would not help the Jews, no matter what!

Months passed. The generals of the Israeli army had a meeting about how to get the stubborn Egyptian officer to start talking. At the meeting, one general said, "Until now, we've been acting tough with Gamal, but that has not worked. Let's try something different. Maybe if we are nice to him, then he will talk to us and give us the information we need."

"That's a good idea," agreed the other generals. "It's certainly worth a try!"

Koby, an important Israeli officer was now in charge of Gamal. "Take him out of prison for a few hours," the generals told him. "Walk with him through the streets of Tel Aviv. Sit down and drink coffee together. Maybe then he'll begin to trust you."

Koby went to the prison and said to Gamal, "Get dressed in regular clothes. We're going to spend the evening together, outside of jail. But be careful. There will be many undercover policemen (policemen dressed as regular people) who will stand near us, so don't even think of running away!"

The Egyptian officer was very excited to leave the prison. "I'll get ready as quickly as I can!" he said.

Koby took Gamal around the city of Tel Aviv. Koby wanted him to see things that he had never seen before. Since it was Chanukah, Koby took him to a big *shul* to see the menorah lighting together with hundreds of people. Koby and Gamal watched as the fires were lit, and listened as *Ha-neiros Halalu* and *Ma'oz Tzur* were sung.

In the middle of the beautiful singing, the Egyptian officer turned to Koby and said, "I remember these words from somewhere! Where have I heard them before?" Suddenly, there was a loud bang. The Egyptian officer had fainted on the floor! Doctors rushed over to help him. The undercover policemen ran toward him too. "Why did he faint?" they all wondered.

When Gamal woke up, he began to talk to the Israeli officers for the first time in months. "I remember my father lighting the menorah when I was a little boy," he began. "We used to sing those exact same words!"

Koby was very surprised. "How can that be?" he asked. "Aren't you an Arab?"

"I always thought I was an Arab," said the Egyptian. "You see, when I was a little boy, my parents were in a terrible car accident and they both died. An Arab family brought me home and took care of me. Since I was so young when the accident happened, I hardly remember my parents. I just assumed that they were also Arabs.

"But tonight," continued Gamal, "when I saw the menorah, I was reminded of the menorah that my parents lit so many years ago. Now I realize that I must be a Jew!"

The Egyptian officer was no longer interested in helping the Arab leaders. Instead, he wanted to help his fellow Jews! Gamal spent hours telling the Israeli soldiers all the secrets that they wanted to know. Slowly but surely, he learned all that he wanted to know about being a Jew.

A few years later, the Israeli army allowed the Arab prisoners to return to Egypt. But Gamal Kareem didn't return with them. He stayed in Eretz Yisrael so that he could live as a Jew.

Every year, when Gamal would light his menorah, he'd remember the special Chanukah in Tel Aviv that brought him back to a life of Torah and *mitzvos*.

CHAPTER 6

For the Love of a Mitzvah

Ilya was a sixth-grade boy who learned in a Shuvu school. Shuvu schools are *frum* schools for children from Russian families who live in Eretz Yisrael.

Ilya's parents had moved to Eretz Yisrael from Russia. Even though they didn't know much about *Yiddishkeit*, they decided to send their son to a Shuvu school so that he could learn about Torah and *mitzvos*.

Since Ilya's parents spoke only Russian and not Hebrew, they could not find jobs in Eretz Yisrael, and so they were very poor. But they loved their son and did whatever they could to make him happy. When Ilya learned about Shabbos, he taught his parents everything he learned, and the family soon began keeping Shabbos. When Ilya learned the *halachos* of kosher food, the family soon began keeping kosher.

Every Chanukah, Ilya set up a menorah in his apartment. Ilya would light the menorah for his family since he was the only one who knew how to say the *berachos* in Hebrew.

Ilya was a good student who always came to school on time. One day, he came a few minutes late. The next day, he was late again. This continued for a few days until it was *erev* Chanukah. That day, the principal noticed that not only was Ilya late, but he was also huffing and puffing as if he had been running for a long time.

"I wonder what's going on with Ilya," said the principal to himself. He called Ilya into his office. "Is everything all right?" he asked.

"Yes," answered Ilya. "Everything is fine."

"I noticed that you've been coming late to school these past few days," said the principal. "You seem to be out of breath from running. Have you been missing the bus?"

Ilya looked down. "Please don't be angry with me," he said. "You'll see — I won't be late anymore." Then he looked up at the principal and explained, "Last week, my Rebbi taught us that it's best to light the menorah with olive oil. I never knew that. We always lit our menorah with candles.

"I know that my parents don't have extra money to buy olive oil so I thought of a plan. Every day this week, when my mother gave me money for the bus ride to school, I didn't spend it. Instead, I put the money in my pocket and went to school by foot. I've been saving up my bus money to buy oil for the menorah.

"Please forgive me for coming late," continued Ilya. "It takes me forty minutes to run to school. But starting from tomorrow, I'll be in school on time. Now that I have enough money to buy oil, I'll be able to start riding the bus again."

Of course, the principal did not punish Ilya for coming late to school. He was amazed that a young boy would give up his bus ride in order to buy oil to light the menorah. The principal put his arm around Ilya's shoulder and said, "I'm so proud of you! In the times of the Chanukah story, Hashem showed His love for the Jewish People by making a *neis* with the menorah. Today, you showed your love for Hashem by working so hard to light the menorah in the best possible way!"

עַל הַנִּסִּים וְעַל הַפֻּרְקָן
וְעַל הַגְּבוּרוֹת וְעַל הַתְּשׁוּעוֹת
וְעַל הַמִּלְחָמוֹת שֶׁעָשִׂיתָ לַאֲבוֹתֵינוּ
בַּיָּמִים הָהֵם בַּזְּמַן הַזֶּה

Acknowledgments

LIGHTS ON THE TRAIN, p. 34
Source: Rabbi Shimon Apisdorf
aish.com

SAVING LIVES, p. 36
Source: *Light One Candle*
Published by Oxford University Press
Also: *Visas for Life*
Published by Edu-Comm Plus

CHANUKAH IN BERGEN BELSEN, p. 39
Source: *Hasidic Tales of the Holocaust*
Published by Oxford University Press and Vintage Books

A YOUNG BOY'S PRECIOUS MENORAH, p. 42
Source: *Small Miracles for the Jewish Heart*
Published by Adams Media Corporation

ARMY SECRETS, p. 45
Source: Rabbi Nachman Seltzer

FOR THE LOVE OF A MITZVAH, p. 48
Source: Shuvu Archives

Glossary

The following glossary provides a partial explanation of some of the Hebrew and Yiddish (Y.) words and phrases used in this book. The spellings and explanations reflect the way the specific word is used herein. Often, there are alternate spellings and meanings for the words.

al kiddush Hashem: for sanctification of the Divine Name; martyrdom.

aveirah: a sin; transgression.

avodah: the service performed in the BEIS HAMIKDASH.

avodah zarah: idol-worship.

bas kol: a Divine voice.

BaYamim HaHeim: lit., "in those days"; a phrase from the *Al HaNisim* prayer.

BaZman HaZeh: lit., "in our times": a phrase from the *Al HaNisim* prayer.

Beis HaMikdash: the Holy Temple in Jerusalem.

berachah (berachos–pl.): blessing(s).

Bnei Yisrael: the children of Israel, i.e. the Jewish People.

bris milah: the ritual of circumcision.

Chachamim: wise men; our Sages.

chutzpah: disrespect; audacity; arrogance.

daven(ed): (Y.) pray(ed).

dreidel: a four-sided spinning top used in a Chanukah game.

eigel ha-zahav: the golden calf.

erev: lit., "evening"; the day preceding a Sabbath or Festival.

frum: religious; observant.

gelt: (Y.) money.

halachos: specific Jewish laws.

Har HaBayis: the Temple Mount.

Heichal: the Temple chamber.

kehunah gedolah: the high priesthood.

keilim: vessels.

Kodesh HaKodashim: the Holy of Holies; the most inner room of the BEIS HAMIKDASH.

kohen (kohanim–pl.): member(s) of the priestly tribe; direct descendant(s) of Aharon.

kohen gadol: the high priest.

korban(os): offering(s) or sacrifice(s) brought in the Holy Temple.

latkes: potato pancakes, traditionally eaten on Chanukah.

malachim: angels.

mesiras nefesh: lit., "giving over one's life"; self-sacrifice; dedication.

midrashim: teachings of the Sages.

mitzvos: Torah commandments.

mizbe'ach: an altar; the holy altar of the Holy Temple.

neis: a miracle.

neshamah: a soul.

pach shemen: a flask of oil.

paroches: the curtain that separates the HEICHAL from the KODESH HAKODASHIM.

rasha (resha'im–pl.): a wicked person; an evil person.

rebbi (rebbeim–pl.): Torah teacher(s).

Rosh Chodesh: the first day of a Hebrew month.

sefarim: holy books.

shamash: the "attendant" candle that is used to light the other flames in the menorah.

Shamayim: Heaven.

shofar: a ram's horn, blown on Rosh Hashanah.

shul: a synagogue.

shulchan: the showbread table in the HEICHAL.

tahor: ritually pure.

talmidim: students; disciples.

tamei: ritually impure.

tefillah: a prayer.

Torah she-b'al peh: the Oral Law.

tzaddik(im–pl.): a righteous, holy person.

tzadekes: a righteous, pious woman.

Yiddishkeit: Judaism.

Yom Tov: lit., a good day; a Jewish holiday.

מָעוֹז צוּר יְשׁוּעָתִי, לְךָ נָאֶה לְשַׁבֵּחַ,
תִּכּוֹן בֵּית תְּפִלָּתִי, וְשָׁם תּוֹדָה נְזַבֵּחַ,
לְעֵת תָּכִין מַטְבֵּחַ מִצָּר הַמְנַבֵּחַ,
אָז אֶגְמֹר בְּשִׁיר מִזְמוֹר, חֲנֻכַּת הַמִּזְבֵּחַ:

רָעוֹת שָׂבְעָה נַפְשִׁי, בְּיָגוֹן כֹּחִי כִּלָּה,
חַיַּי מֵרְרוּ בְקֹשִׁי, בְּשִׁעְבּוּד מַלְכוּת עֶגְלָה,
וּבְיָדוֹ הַגְּדוֹלָה, הוֹצִיא אֶת הַסְּגֻלָּה,
חֵיל פַּרְעֹה, וְכָל־זַרְעוֹ, יָרְדוּ כְּאֶבֶן בִּמְצוּלָה:

דְּבִיר קָדְשׁוֹ הֱבִיאַנִי, וְגַם שָׁם לֹא שָׁקַטְתִּי,
וּבָא נוֹגֵשׂ וְהִגְלַנִי, כִּי זָרִים עָבַדְתִּי,
וְיֵין רַעַל מָסַכְתִּי, כִּמְעַט שֶׁעָבַרְתִּי,
קֵץ בָּבֶל, זְרֻבָּבֶל, לְקֵץ שִׁבְעִים נוֹשַׁעְתִּי:

כְּרֹת קוֹמַת בְּרוֹשׁ בִּקֵּשׁ, אֲגָגִי בֶּן־הַמְּדָתָא,
וְנִהְיְתָה לוֹ לְפַח וּלְמוֹקֵשׁ, וְגַאֲוָתוֹ נִשְׁבָּתָה,
רֹאשׁ יְמִינִי נִשֵּׂאתָ, וְאוֹיֵב שְׁמוֹ מָחִיתָ,
רֹב בָּנָיו, וְקִנְיָנָיו, עַל הָעֵץ תָּלִיתָ:

יְוָנִים נִקְבְּצוּ עָלַי, אֲזַי בִּימֵי חַשְׁמַנִּים,
וּפָרְצוּ חוֹמוֹת מִגְדָּלַי, וְטִמְּאוּ כָּל הַשְּׁמָנִים,
וּמִנּוֹתַר קַנְקַנִּים, נַעֲשָׂה נֵס לַשּׁוֹשַׁנִּים,
בְּנֵי בִינָה, יְמֵי שְׁמוֹנָה, קָבְעוּ שִׁיר וּרְנָנִים:

חֲשׂוֹף זְרוֹעַ קָדְשֶׁךָ, וְקָרֵב קֵץ הַיְשׁוּעָה,
נְקֹם נִקְמַת דַּם עֲבָדֶיךָ, מֵאֻמָּה הָרְשָׁעָה,
כִּי אָרְכָה לָנוּ הַיְשׁוּעָה, וְאֵין קֵץ לִימֵי הָרָעָה,
דְּחֵה אַדְמוֹן, בְּצֵל צַלְמוֹן, הָקֵם לָנוּ רוֹעִים שִׁבְעָה:

בָּרוּךְ אַתָּה ה׳
אֱלֹקֵינוּ מֶלֶךְ הָעוֹלָם,
אֲשֶׁר קִדְּשָׁנוּ בְּמִצְוֹתָיו
וְצִוָּנוּ לְהַדְלִיק נֵר
שֶׁל חֲנֻכָּה:

בָּרוּךְ אַתָּה ה׳
אֱלֹקֵינוּ מֶלֶךְ הָעוֹלָם,
שֶׁעָשָׂה נִסִּים לַאֲבוֹתֵינוּ
בַּיָּמִים הָהֵם בַּזְּמַן הַזֶּה:

On the first night add:

בָּרוּךְ אַתָּה ה׳ אֱלֹקֵינוּ מֶלֶךְ הָעוֹלָם,
שֶׁהֶחֱיָנוּ וְקִיְּמָנוּ וְהִגִּיעָנוּ לַזְּמַן הַזֶּה:

הַנֵּרוֹת הַלָּלוּ אֲנַחְנוּ מַדְלִיקִין
עַל הַנִּסִּים, וְעַל הַנִּפְלָאוֹת, וְעַל הַתְּשׁוּעוֹת,
וְעַל הַמִּלְחָמוֹת, שֶׁעָשִׂיתָ לַאֲבוֹתֵינוּ בַּיָּמִים הָהֵם
בַּזְּמַן הַזֶּה, עַל־יְדֵי כֹּהֲנֶיךָ הַקְּדוֹשִׁים,
וְכָל שְׁמוֹנַת יְמֵי חֲנֻכָּה הַנֵּרוֹת הַלָּלוּ קֹדֶשׁ הֵם,
וְאֵין לָנוּ רְשׁוּת לְהִשְׁתַּמֵּשׁ בָּהֶם, אֶלָּא לִרְאוֹתָם בִּלְבָד
כְּדֵי לְהוֹדוֹת וּלְהַלֵּל לְשִׁמְךָ הַגָּדוֹל
עַל־נִסֶּיךָ וְעַל־נִפְלְאוֹתֶיךָ וְעַל־יְשׁוּעָתֶךָ: